195

KU-441-333

Net-Making & Knotting

LITTLE
CRAFT BOOK
SERIES

By Warren M. Hartzell & Lura LaBarge

STERLING PUBLISHING CO., INC. NEW YORK

Oak Tree Press Co., Ltd.   London & Sydney

SAUNDERS OF TORONTO, Ltd., Don Mills, Canada

Little Craft Book Series

Metric Conversion Chart

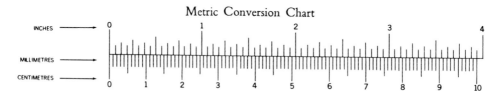

Copyright © 1974 by Sterling Publishing Co., Inc. 419 Park Avenue South, New York, N.Y. 10016
Distributed in Canada by Saunders of Toronto, Ltd., Don Mills, Ontario
British edition published by Oak Tree Press Co., Ltd., Nassau, Bahamas
Distributed in Australia and New Zealand by Oak Tree Press Co., Ltd.,
P.O. Box J34, Brickfield Hill, Sydney 2000, N.S.W.
Distributed in the United Kingdom and elsewhere in the British Commonwealth
by Ward Lock Ltd., 116 Baker Street, London W 1
Manufactured in the United States of America   *All rights reserved*
Library of Congress Catalog Card No.: 74–82328
Sterling ISBN 0–8069–5310–1 Trade   Oak Tree 7061–2039–6
5311–X Library

Contents

Before You Begin

Net-making is a systematic method of knotting, in which you repeat the same hand-tied knot row after row to create a fabric from one strand or cord. In this, netting is somewhat similar to crocheting or knitting in that you work back into the previous row to form a continuous whole.

Though perhaps most often associated with fishing, netting is certainly not limited to fish nets. Because of its strength and lightness, net is a natural choice for carriers and containers and can also be used to make many other useful and decorative items. With the widespread interest in crafts, soft sculpture and fabric constructions, the creative possibilities based on the net-making technique are innumerable. The aim of this book is to acquaint you with some of these possibilities.

You achieve variety in netting depending on the cords you use, their size and on the size of the mesh (the loop or space between any two knots). By increasing and decreasing, seaming and manipulating shapes, you can use netting to create a variety of forms. By combining netting with other knotted techniques, such as macramé, you may discover entirely new creative directions.

Perhaps one reason net-making is not thought of immediately as a decorative art is the lack of color in most examples. You can easily remedy this by using the colorful macramé cords available in craft and hobby shops or by using cotton seine twine which you can dye with cold-water or washing-machine dyes.

If you do want to dye your own cord, you must first decide when to do the dyeing. If you dye the cord before you make your net, you may have short pieces of odd-colored cord left over. When you use dyed cord for tassels later, you very seldom get good results. The dye has not penetrated well so you get a striped effect. Of course, not every project has tassels, and it is often advantageous to dye various sizes of cord at one time.

You may also dye the piece after it is finished, but note that it may shrink considerably and if the knots ever loosen, you will see the original color, where the dye did not penetrate. Tassels, though, will be dyed all the way through.

Whenever you decide to dye, first wash the cord or finished net in quite hot water, using detergent and, if you like, fabric softener. Rinse extremely well and follow the directions of the manufacturer of the commercial dyes.

Equipment and Tools

Cord or Twine

A few twines are made specifically for hand-netting. Bonded nylon is one. Normally, nylon is slippery and does not easily hold a knot, but the bonding process helps. Cotton seine twine is most useful for net-making, but you may want lighter weights too. Finding sizes 18 and 21 is easy, but finding smaller sizes may present a problem. You may find #12 cotton seine twine in hardware stores, but you might have to look for #9; #6 is made, but mostly for commercial users.

You may also net with various types of craft cords and yarns. Look for marine suppliers, hardware stores, craft shops and upholstery and weaving supply houses who carry suitable cords.

Another thing to consider in your twine selection is, of course, use. Salt water is harder on nets than fresh water, and direct sunshine is worst of all. Washing off slime as quickly as possible helps preserve the nets. You might also want to consider using some of the commercial preservatives recommended for cotton canvas for outdoor accessories.

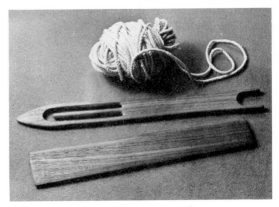

Illus. 1. Wooden shuttle (top) and gauge.

Shuttle and Gauge

Though it is possible to net without a shuttle and gauge, it is easier and more efficient to use these tools (see Illus. 1). The shuttle is the wooden, plastic or even bone holder of twine or cord which you use to carry the twine while making the netting knot. The width of the gauge determines the size of the mesh. Using a gauge ensures that the mesh will be uniform and a specific size.

Gauges actually measure just under the size you think they are. That is, a $1''$ gauge is really about $\frac{15}{16}''$ wide. When you are first learning to net, try out a few different sizes, one size to a row, and measure the results. When you become more proficient, you can try double wrapping a gauge to make a mesh loop twice as big as the one you expect from that gauge.

If you cannot find a shuttle at your local crafts supplier, through fishermen's suppliers in your area, or by mail order, you can easily make your own. In fact, some net-makers prefer to make their own tools.

To make a shuttle, choose a hardwood that you can polish reasonably well, so that the cord does not catch on the shuttle. About $\frac{1}{4}''$ thick is the thickest a shuttle can be and still handle easily; $\frac{3}{16}''$ thick is better and $\frac{1}{8}''$-thick boxwood or fine-grained straight maple is ideal. The shuttle and gauges shown in this book are walnut and were made with simple hand and power tools. You can use hand tools—in fact, a jackknife plus a bit of sandpaper are enough—but a power jig saw is faster. The pattern in Illus. 2A and 2B is for the most common shuttle shape, though by no means the only shape.

To make a shuttle like the one shown in Illus. 2A and 2B, trace the parts of the pattern. It is sized for use with gauges $1''$ and larger. If you want to use smaller gauges, reduce the size of the shuttle which should always be somewhat narrower than the gauge you are using. The pattern is drawn on a grid so that you can reduce or enlarge it easily.

5

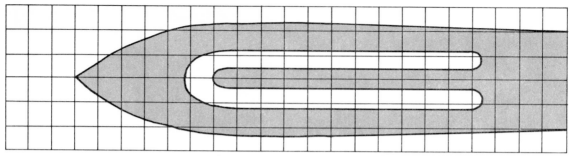

Illus. 2A. Shuttle pattern.

The length of a shuttle depends on two things: maintaining reasonable proportions so it handles well and the size cord you are using. Heavy cord wound many times on a short shuttle is not going to go through the meshes as easily as the same amount of cord wound on a longer shuttle. The pattern given produces a shuttle $10\frac{1}{2}''$ long that will carry about 15 yards of #18 twine or 12 yards of #36.

Other Equipment

In addition, you need a work surface into which you can drive a few nails. This can be an old wooden desk or simply be a piece of $1'' \times 2''$ wood, and a C-clamp to clamp the board onto a work table. The exact angle into which you clamp such a work board depends entirely on which angle you will feel most comfortable with. This can mean flat on the work table, at a slightly raised angle, or even up on a wall, perpendicular to the work table. Try a few work positions to see which you prefer.

You may also use a wooden dowel, instead of a work board, which you attach to the edge of your work table with two C-clamps.

You also need scissors, occasionally a raffia needle, a good light and a comfortable chair.

Illus. 2B. Shuttle pattern.

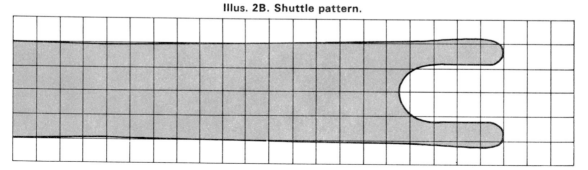

Diamond Mesh Carrier

Materials:
    #36 cotton seine twine
    3″ gauge

A rectangular sample of diamond meshing is an appropriate first project to acquaint you with the basic net-making tools and techniques. Finding something useful to do with such a rectangle is not hard at all. For example, you can put the piece down flat and pile it full of clothes to take to a rummage sale. Or, you can tie through the mesh and you will have an easily handled bundle. If you put down your sample in the woods and gather firewood, you can tie it and tote it back to the campsite. An improvement is a double selvage edge (see instructions on page 12) if you know you are always going to hook or tie down the net through the edges. For your first project, why not make a rectangular car-top carrier, as shown in Illus. 3? Make a net larger than 5 feet by 5 feet.

Filling the Shuttle

Either use the shuttle you just made (page 6) or select one slightly smaller than the width of the gauge you will be using most. Filling the shuttle properly is the first step.

If you are using the style shuttle in Illus. 2A and 2B, hold it in your hand. Hold the free end of twine under your thumb. Bring the twine up around the tongue and down under the heel, holding down the free end as you go (see Illus. 4, left). Turn the shuttle over in your hand and carry the twine up, around the tongue, and back

Illus. 3. A rectangular car-top carrier.

down to the heel (see Illus. 4, right). Turn the shuttle again and continue in this manner until it is full, but not so heavily loaded as to hamper passing it through the mesh loops.

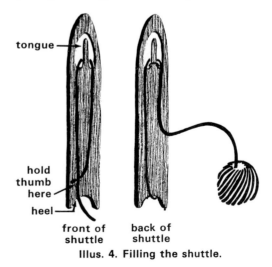

tongue —

hold
thumb
here —

heel —

front of
shuttle

back of
shuttle

Illus. 4. Filling the shuttle.

7

You may find that some cords kink up as you take them from the ball. Cords you have dyed yourself often do so. Do not wind the kinks onto the shuttle. Instead, hold the cord as it comes from the ball and let the shuttle fall free so it can rotate, unkinking the cord before you wind it.

Double Headrope Start to Cast-On

You always tie the netting knot into a loop or mesh from a casting-on process of some kind or from the previous row. You must have a loop of some sort to tie the knot. Netting is worked from left to right. Starting from a double headrope permits you to preview the netting knot. It is also

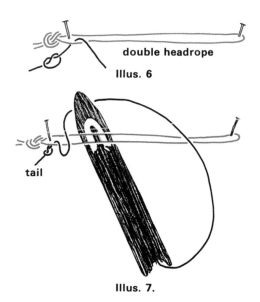

double headrope

Illus. 6

tail

Illus. 7.

a reasonably easy beginning which you can transfer to a dowel after the second row for greater ease in turning the work, so that it is possible to work from left to right.

To make the double headrope, you need a piece of #36 seine twine about 12″ long. Make a loop and tie the ends together with a double overhand knot (see Illus. 5). Drive two nails into your work board so you can stretch the loop between them as shown in Illus. 6. Clamp the board in working position (see page 6).

Tie an overhand knot (see Illus. 5) towards the end of the cord coming from the filled shuttle. The length free beyond this knot is the "tail." The cord from the shuttle is the "shuttle cord." Hold the knot under the double headrope and take the shuttle up through the loop, bringing the knot beneath the double headrope.

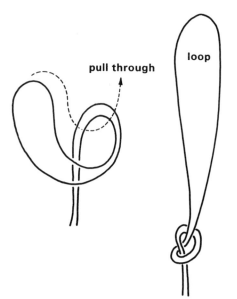

pull through

loop

Illus. 5. Double overhand knot.

Hold the knot there by the tail and pinch the cord as it comes through the loop between your thumb and forefinger. Throw the cord in a loop over the headrope as shown in Illus. 7. Take the shuttle under *both* parts of the headrope loop and over the cord just thrown. Pull the shuttle through the loop and down, letting up on the pinching so the knot forms on the double headrope as shown in Illus. 8.

Now use the 3″ gauge. Hold the gauge up under the headrope so the shuttle cord falls across the front of it. Bring the shuttle up behind the gauge and through the headrope loop as shown in Illus. 8. Repeat the pinch, throw the cord in a loop, take the shuttle under *both* sides of the headrope loop and over the thrown rope. Pull to form another knot alongside the first one.

Continue repeating this until you have 9 or 10 loops around the gauge. Remove the gauge stick. All the loops should be the same size. Lift the headrope off the nails and turn it over, end for end, so what was at the left end facing you in Illus. 8 is at the right end facing away from you in Illus. 9. Now you are ready for the netting knot.

The Netting Knot

By turning the headrope end for end, you also bring the shuttle cord to the left side and you are ready to commence the first row of netting knots. Let the cord from the shuttle come in front of your gauge. Hold the gauge up to the bottom of the mesh above. Take the shuttle behind the gauge and up through the first loop as shown in

Illus. 8.

Illus. 9.

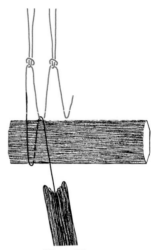

Illus. 10, coming towards you from the back of the loop to the front. Pull the shuttle towards you to bring the cord snugly around the gauge (see Illus. 11). Remember, the purpose of the gauge is to create uniform mesh. If you tighten one time and relax the next, the mesh will not be the same size.

Hold the cord down to the front of the gauge with your thumb. Hold the gauge tight up against the loop above and throw a loop from the shuttle over the back of your left hand. Now put the shuttle behind *both* sides of the loop mesh you just came through (see Illus. 12). Take the shuttle over the loop you threw from the shuttle.

Now comes the tricky part. Pinch as you pull the shuttle cord tightly and roll your left thumb up to make the knot form at the top of the gauge (see Illus. 13). The trick is in pinching the loop above the gauge and the held shuttle cord until just the right moment, and then rolling your thumb just

Illus. 11.

enough. Practice until your knot looks like the one shown in Illus. 13.

Work two rows. At this point, you may wish to remove the headrope and insert a dowel. Then continue knot-making for a total of 9 or 10 rows.

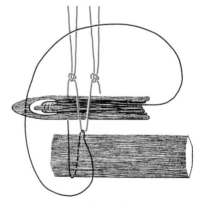

Illus. 12.

10

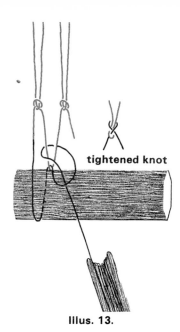

tightened knot

Illus. 13.

shown in Illus. 16A to 16C. Keep the joining knot away from the middle of a mesh. Some joining knots are stronger than others, and some are preferable where appearance is important.

Joining Knots

The simplest joining knot is the double over-hand knot (see Illus. 5). You can use this knot for practically anything, but it makes a large, unattractive clump when you are using larger size cords.

The next most easily tied knot is an overhand knot in the old end, encircled with an overhand knot in the new shuttle cord (see Illus. 16A). Although this knot is not very strong, it is quite tidy.

You can make a better join by tying the netting knot as usual, but by first placing the new shuttle cord over the mesh to be netted into, backing it up with a single overhand knot (see Illus. 16B).

You can make an even stronger and more attractive join by loosening up the last netting knot you tied and by threading the new shuttle cord back through it, stopping both ends with an overhand knot (see Illus. 16C).

Refilling the Shuttle

When you use up the twine on your shuttle, wind more twine onto the shuttle. Join the old and new ends with one or another of the knots

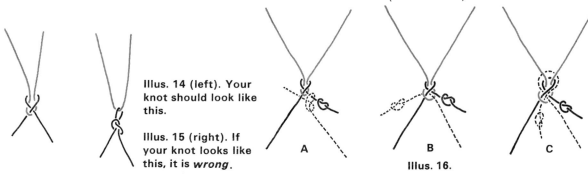

Illus. 14 (left). Your knot should look like this.

Illus. 15 (right). If your knot looks like this, it is *wrong*.

A   B   C

Illus. 16.

11

Tie-Off

When you have completed 9 or 10 rows of netting, you need to tie off the twine to complete your rectangular carrier. The easiest and simplest way to do this is to tie an overhand knot—or two, if you feel this is necessary for strength—into the shuttle cord, working the knot tight up against the last netting knot. Then, simply cut off the cord.

Double Selvage

A double selvage is one way for you to finish off the edge of this carrier after you have completed netting.

To make a double selvage, re-wind your shuttle so it carries two cords as one. Using the netting knot, tie onto any perimeter mesh loop at the middle of the loop, leaving one tail at least 12" long, the other not less than 6". Work around the edge of the net using the 3" gauge, making netting knots, with the double cord handled as one cord. When your shuttle is empty, refill it and join as

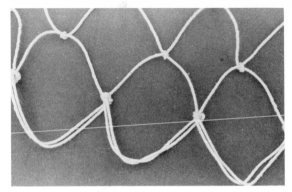

Illus. 17. Double selvage.

shown in Illus. 18. Join the short end of the new shuttle cord with one end of the old cord at the netting knot where shown. Work back the 12" tail from the new shuttle cord and join it with the other old cord at the previous netting knot. This puts joiner knots on two consecutive meshes. Then, continue knotting your double selvage as previously.

When you have completed the edge, slacken off the first knot you tied and run one ending cord through that knot. Take the 12" tail back to the next knot and join it and the other double cord there, in much the same way as you joined a new shuttle cord. This way, you place smaller joining knots at two different meshes.

You have now completed your first net. Use it to prevent loose, light things from being blown away. If you use it as a car-top carrier, as shown in Illus. 3, fasten the net securely to your car's luggage rack or rails with rope or elastic luggage tie-downs.

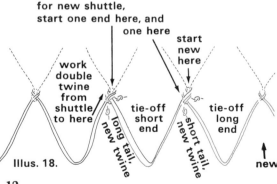

for new shuttle, start one end here, and one here

start new here

work double twine from shuttle to here

tie-off short end

long tail, new twine

tie-off long end

short tail, new twine

Illus. 18.

new doubled twine, long tail worked back through

Book Bag

Materials:
   #18 cotton seine twine
   two $\frac{3}{8}''$ wooden dowels, each 10" long
   $1\frac{1}{2}''$ gauge
   3" gauge
   short piece of button thread

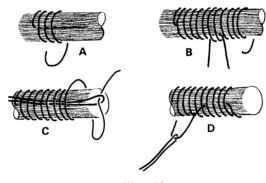

Illus. 19.

Another simple project you can make from a single rectangle of diamond meshing is a book bag. The one shown in Illus. 41 is just the right size for a library pick-up and delivery trip. You can easily make a larger or smaller carrier by adding or subtracting mesh or by increasing or decreasing the gauge size.

First, you need to make the net. Using the double headrope method, cast on 8 mesh using a 3" gauge. Then, using the $1\frac{1}{2}''$ gauge, work two rows and transfer to a dowel stick, if you wish. Work a total of 12 rows, the last one on the 3" gauge. Tie off as described on page 12.

To complete the bag, first sand and stain the ends of the dowels to give them an attractive finish. Then hold one end of twine against the dowel as shown in Illus. 19A. Commence wrapping over it about $\frac{1}{4}''$ from the end of the dowel, fastening the twine down. Wrap five or six turns, and then wrap through the first mesh loop across the end of the net, as shown in Illus. 19B. Wrap through each mesh loop twice. Continue to wrap, catching mesh loops as you go. Be sure to space the loops evenly, but leave a wider space at the middle of the dowel for a hand hold. You might find it helpful to work out the spacing first, mark-ing the position of each mesh connection on the dowel, picking up each mesh as you come to the mark.

Towards the end of the dowel, lay a piece of strong thread (button thread is good) in a loop as shown in Illus. 19C. Wrap the twine tightly over the thread to the end of the dowel, less the same $\frac{1}{4}''$ as you left at the first end wrapped. Run the end of the twine through the captive loop. Pull the

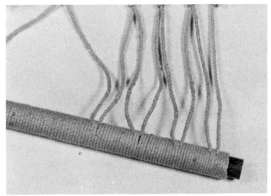

Illus. 20. Wrapping through the mesh loops to form the handle.

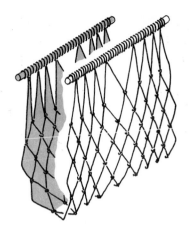

Illus. 21.

thread loop hard, bringing the end of the twine down under the wrapping and through to free the thread (see Illus. 19D). Glue the end and cut it off close to the wrapping.

Do the same with the other dowel at the other end of the net. Then fold in the rectangle in the middle, bringing the two dowels alongside each other (see Illus. 21). With short pieces of twine, encircle the end mesh of the top side and the end knot of the other side. Tie a square knot and over-hand knots in either end of the twine pieces (see Illus. 22). Do this on both ends of the bag.

With this simple method, you close up the end seams to keep the books in. The stiff, straight dowels enable the bag to be opened easily for inserting straight, flat books, tablets, or anything else of similar proportions.

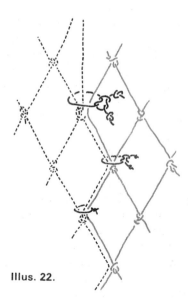

Illus. 22.

14

Tennis Bag

Materials:
   #9 cotton seine twine
   12 plastic or bone rings, $\frac{1}{2}''$ in diameter
   #72 cotton seine twine
   $\frac{3}{4}''$ gauge
   $1\frac{1}{2}''$ gauge

The neatest way to start this bag (see photograph on back cover) or any circular piece from the bottom is the grommet start. To do this, first fill your shuttle with the #9 twine. Then make an overhand knot around the descending tail as shown in Illus. 23. Tighten the knot and hang it on a nail as shown. Hold the $\frac{3}{4}''$ gauge under the knot and take the shuttle cord over the front and around the back of the gauge just as you did for the netting knot. Bring the shuttle between the two parts of the hanging loop (just as you come through the two parts of the hanging mesh loop for the netting knot) (see Illus. 24). Hold with your thumb and forefinger at the top of the gauge stick.

Throw a loop to the left (just as for the netting knot). Take the shuttle behind both parts of the hanging loop and over the thrown loop. Pull the shuttle cord to the right and downward (see Illus. 25). Cast on 13 loops in this way. Remove the gauge.

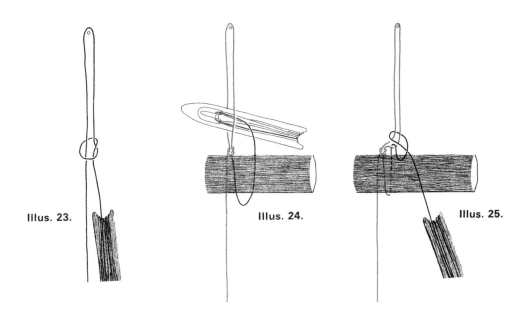

Illus. 23.   Illus. 24.   Illus. 25.

15

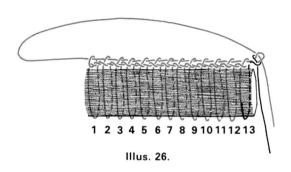

1 2 3 4 5 6 7 8 9 10 11 12 13

Illus. 26.

Take the grommet starting loop off the nail and put the tail through that loop (see Illus. 26). Pull on the tail until that loop tightens around it, thus forming the circular grommet and bringing the tail and the shuttle cord adjacent to each other so you can tie them together tight against the grommet ring as shown in Illus. 27. Pull hard to make the starting loops slide over the tail cord, but make sure you put the end of the tail through the loop first in case the starting loops move all of a sudden and you lose the loop.

Now tie the shuttle cord to the tail, as shown in Illus. 27, thus forming the 14th loop around the grommet. The best knot to use for this is an overhand knot around the tail, tied tightly with the shuttle cord. You can also, as shown, tie a double overhand knot in the two cords, which is more secure. It is also possible to join the tail and shuttle cord with a netting knot tied with the

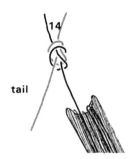

tail

Illus. 27.

Illus. 28 (right). Rotating arrangement to facilitate working from a grommet.

shuttle cord around the tail. Whichever method you use to tie the tail and shuttle cord, the 14th loop must be the same size as the other 13.

Once you have the grommet formed and tied together, you can facilitate working from it if you use some sort of freely rotating arrangement. The simplest method is to put a $\frac{1}{4}''$ bolt first through a washer (so the grommet does not slip over the bolt head), then through the grommet, and then through another washer. Fit the bolt through a hole in a support of some kind. (Illus. 28 shows a piece of $1'' \times 2''$ wood screwed to a board that was then clamped to the work table.) Add another washer and two nuts. The second nut locks the bolt by jamming up tightly to the first nut so the bolt can turn freely. (You could use a lock washer instead of the jam nut method.) Now, the grommet can rotate freely, held by the bolt, as you work on it and is easy to remove when you are done. You can, of course, just put the grommet over a nail and work flat from that, but a horizontal pivot works better.

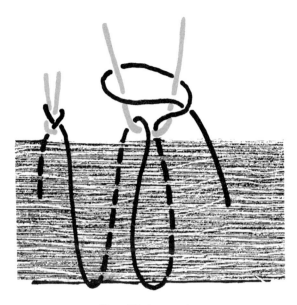

Illus. 29. Increasing.

The Bag Itself

You now have 14 loops ready to be worked. Keep only three loops at a time on the gauge as you work. Start with the gauge stick held under loop #1 as shown in Illus. 29. You always want a straight pull from the central point of the grommet to maintain a neat, even net. Slip one loop off one end of the gauge each time you form a new one at the other end.

Work around, netting once into each loop formed by the grommet. This is row 1. Work row 2 into those loops you formed by knotting row 1. Increase in the 2nd, 3rd, 4th, 5th and 6th meshes.

Increasing

To increase, hold the gauge to the loop of the previous row as for a regular netting knot. Bring the shuttle cord over and around the gauge and through the loop, then go around the gauge and through the loop *again*. Then proceed to throw the cord over to the left and pull and roll as for a regular netting knot (see Illus. 29).

Knot without increasing into the 7th mesh, increase in the 8th, 9th, 10th, 11th and 12th

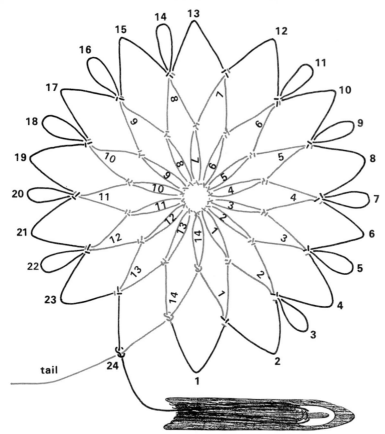

Illus. 30. Increasing from a grommet.

meshes as shown in Illus. 30. Knot without increasing in the 13th loop.

Increasing from a grommet start can present problems if you do not think ahead. Try to avoid increasing in every loop as this would include the loop formed by tying the tail to the shuttle cord and there is no neat way to accomplish this. Also, it is difficult to work through the grommet-type cast-on loops with a full shuttle, so it is best

not to increase until the next row. Then, plan your increases to avoid using the mesh formed by tying and, to keep your net symmetrical, the one directly opposite it (for this project, you therefore did not increase in the 7th mesh). In addition, try not to increase in the loop formed by the increase in the previous row, although this is not always possible.

You form the 24th mesh loop of row 2 when

18

you tie the shuttle cord coming from the knot you just tied in the 13th mesh of the first row with the tail hanging from the 14th mesh in the first row. Study Illus. 30 to make sure you understand how this tail-created-mesh frees you to start the next row around.

Work 25 rows in the circular manner but straight, with no further increases. This is called "working circular straight." On the 26th row, change to the $1\frac{1}{2}''$ gauge and work one row. Tie the shuttle cord to the tail and tie off.

Ring Closing

Gather two mesh at a time and treat as one to attach the 12 rings as shown in Illus. 32. To put a closed ring on the closed mesh loops, first fold the paired mesh loops and lay the ring over it. Pick up the mesh loops and drop them over the lower edge of the ring. Pick up the ring by this edge and shake it so the loop moves around to the opposite side of the ring. A neat "lark's head attachment" is the result. This is a very handy method of attaching bone or plastic rings to the top of a bag you plan to run a drawstring through. Of course, you will not always work with two mesh at a time as you did for this tennis bag.

Drawstring

Cut two lengths of #72 twine, each 3 feet long. To make a double draw closing, run one length of twine through the rings and back to the starting point. Fold the other length in half and with the middle at the start and finish of the first length, run each end of the second length through six rings.

To finish the drawstring, fold back the ends of each set of cords. Then wrap over these ends with twine (see Illus. 31). Pulling on both wrapped sections closes the bag. Pulling on both central points opens it.

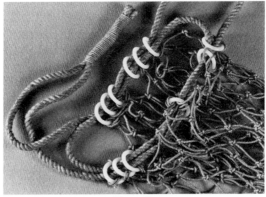

Illus. 31.

Illus. 32.

Hand-Held Fishing Net

Materials:

> #9 cotton seine twine, treated or nylon bonded
> 6 foot-long piece of $\frac{3}{8}''$ aluminum tubing (cut after bending)
> $1'' \times 3'' \times 8''$ piece of oak for handle
> four #4 flat head wood screws, $\frac{7}{8}''$ long (aluminum)
> fence staple
> screw eye and leather thong for handle loop
> $\frac{3}{4}''$ gauge
> $1\frac{1}{4}''$ gauge
> $2''$ gauge
> drill and $\frac{3}{32}''$ bit
> chisel or router
> hacksaw

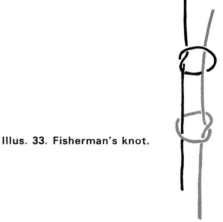

Illus. 33. Fisherman's knot.

Sports fishermen the world over need hand-held landing nets. Making such a net (see Illus. 43) is a good way to practice the grommet start method. If you have an old net frame, you can adapt this net to fit it. If not, make the frame described on page 22. You will no doubt be proud to land that trout in a net you made yourself.

Using the grommet start method, cast on 7 loops over the $\frac{3}{4}''$ gauge. Tying the shuttle cord to the tail makes the eighth loop. In the 2nd row, increase six times to make a total of 14 loops. In the 3rd row, increase four times to make a total of 18 loops. In the 4th row, increase six times to make a total of 24 loops. In the 5th row, increase eight times to make a total of 32 loops. In the 7th row, increase eight times to make a total of 40 loops.

Work straight to the 12th row, using the $\frac{3}{4}''$ gauge. On the 13th row, change to the $1\frac{1}{4}''$ gauge and work straight to the 24th row.

In the course of making this net, you will undoubtedly need to refill the shuttle. You could join the new cord using one of the joining knots described on page 11. From the standpoint of appearance, these knots are probably preferable. Here, where strength rather than appearance matters, you may choose a stronger knot. The fisherman's knot (see Illus. 33), which is simply two overhand knots, each encircling the tail of the other cord, is easy to make and fairly strong.

Change to the $2''$ gauge and fill your shuttle for the double selvage. Work one row of double selvage (see page 12) around the edge. Tie off.

Sizing

So far, you have made projects following the instructions here. You may, however, want to make a bag of a different size than is described. Diamond meshing, which you have been doing, produces a two-way stretch fabric and, consequently, determining sizes is a very approximate thing at best. There are some sizing factors involved, however, and if you understand them, you can arrive at an informed guess as to how many meshes on what size gauge will produce a net capable of containing what you want it to hold. First of all, the size of the twine you use will affect the figures to a degree. Also, you must assume the diamond mesh is going to be used square, which is often not the case, if the mesh are stretched. In addition, you must consider how tight you tie the knots and how heavy the contents of the net will be when determining size. You will have to round off fractions in your calculations.

The chart given here can be used as a guide for sizing net bags, landing nets, and so on. To use the chart, decide the size bag you want to make—either by diameter or circumference. Select the size gauge to use, considering what the bag will contain, and then read down and over to see how many loops you need. If you are making a fish net, *double* the number of loops shown for a full net.

GUIDE FOR SIZING

gauge/diagonal measure when net is square

number of mesh loops for	$\frac{3}{4}''$ gauge $1\frac{1}{16}''$ diagonal	$1''$ gauge $1\frac{7}{16}''$ diagonal	$1\frac{1}{4}''$ gauge $1\frac{3}{4}''$ diagonal	$1\frac{1}{2}''$ gauge $2\frac{1}{8}''$ diagonal	$1\frac{3}{4}''$ gauge $2\frac{1}{2}''$ diagonal	$2''$ gauge $2\frac{13}{16}''$ diagonal	$2\frac{1}{2}''$ gauge $3\frac{9}{16}''$ diagonal
8" diameter or $25\frac{1}{8}''$ circumference	24 loops	18 loops	14 loops	12 loops			
10" diameter or $31\frac{7}{16}''$ circumference	30 loops	22 loops	18 loops	15 loops	13 loops		
12" diameter or $37\frac{11}{16}''$ circumference	35 loops	27 loops	21 loops	18 loops	17 loops	13 loops	
16" diameter or $50\frac{1}{4}''$ circumference			28 loops	24 loops	22 loops	17 loops	16 loops
18" diameter or $56\frac{9}{16}''$ circumference				26 loops	25 loops	19 loops	18 loops
21" diameter or 66" circumference					28 loops	22 loops	21 loops
24" diameter or $75\frac{3}{8}''$ circumference						26 loops	24 loops

Making the Handle

To make the handle, use the pattern for the aluminum frame in Illus. 34. Note that it is drawn on a grid which you must enlarge on

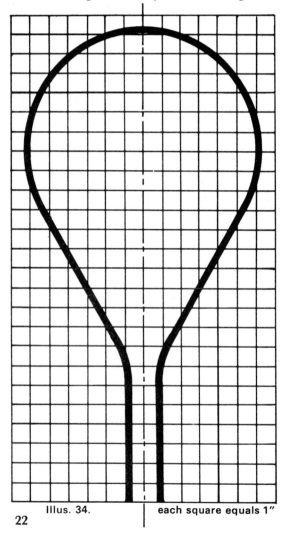

Illus. 34.   each square equals 1″

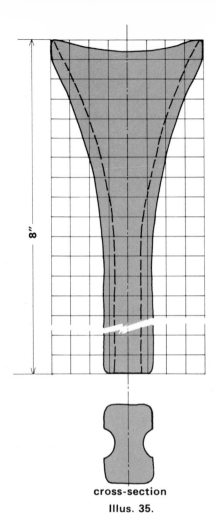

8″

cross-section

Illus. 35.

paper so each square equals 1″. Bend the tubing to conform to the pattern.

A complete pattern for the wooden tongue is given in Illus. 35. Transfer it onto the wood and saw out your 8″-long wood piece accordingly.

Using a chisel, gouge out channels along the edges where shown in the cross-section in Illus. 35. Fit the aluminum frame into these grooves. If you have a router handy, you may make the grooves with it instead of a chisel.

Next, clamp the bent frame to the shaped tongue and drill holes for four screws at intervals along the frame. Cut off the ends of the tubing flush with the end of the wooden tongue. Finish the wooden part with a preservative and/or marine varnish.

Thread the aluminum frame through the double selvage, making sure you thread through both cords of each loop but the last (40th) loop, which you leave loose temporarily.

Fasten the frame to the handle with four screws through the holes you drilled. You may also want to use epoxy glue to fasten the frame securely to the handle. Attach the 40th loop to the end of the tongue with a fence staple. Insert a screw eye in the opposite end of the tongue. Tie the leather thong through the screw eye to create a hanging loop for your net.

You are now ready to land that elusive trout!

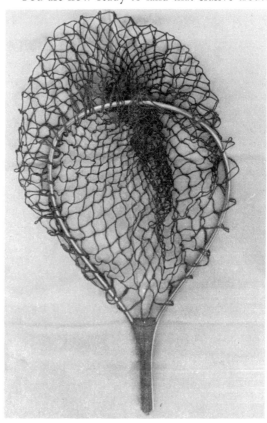

Illus. 37. Completed net.

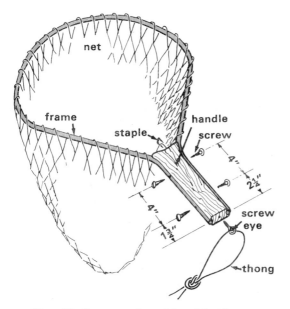

Illus. 36. Construction of hand-held net.

Basketball Net

Materials:

   #72 cotton seine twine
   basketball net frame with a 19″ diameter
   $1\frac{1}{2}$″ gauge
   2″ gauge
   ruler
   piece of string for measuring

Sleeve Netting

For some projects, you may want to work circularly but you cannot begin from a grommet start. If you want to make a bag with a seamed bottom, you do not want a grommet. If you want to make a basketball net, you do not want a grommet either. In such cases, you can start netting from the top and work circularly down to the bottom. Such netting is known as "sleeve netting," because the net you produce is open-ended and circular or tubular, similar to a sleeve. In making a basketball replacement net (see photograph on the front cover), you can net directly on the frame or hoop where it is to be used.

You can also use sleeve netting to make other nets worked on similar frames, though your size and number of mesh may vary with a different style frame.

Tie the measuring string across from one clip on the basketball hoop to the one directly opposite it to find the middle of the hoop. Measure from one side to the other and mark the middle. Securely loop the shuttle cord to a frame clip, leaving a 24″ tail. (If the clips on your basketball hoop do not hold the shuttle cord securely, twist

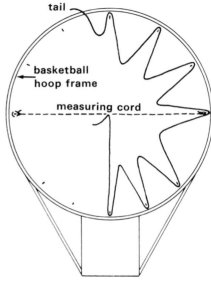

Illus. 38.

and tie each measured loop at each clip to hold it from slipping while you net. Untie the loops when you have completed the net.)

Take the shuttle cord from that clip to the middle point to determine the length of each mesh loop in the first row around the frame (see Illus. 38). Tie the shuttle cord and the tail together when you complete the circuit. Begin netting as described on page 9, working the second row with the 2″ gauge. Net the remaining five rows with the $1\frac{1}{2}$″ gauge. Tie the tail to the shuttle cord to complete this sleeve net. Then tie a single overhand knot tight against each end before you cut off the tail and shuttle to prevent your net from coming untied.

Lamp Cover

Materials:
  soft cable cord, $\frac{3}{32}''$ in diameter
  3″ gauge
  $2\frac{1}{2}''$ gauge
  2″ gauge
  $1\frac{3}{4}''$ gauge
  $1\frac{1}{2}''$ gauge
  scrap piece (about 24″ long) of #21 or #36
    seine twine

If you are working on something that has no frame, you can also start sleeve netting from a single headrope formed into a working loop, which may or may not be a part of the finished net.

While you are experimenting, also consider using other cords besides seine twine. Soft cable cord is easy to handle, soft to touch and, because it is bright white, takes dye well too. In netting, it unravels more easily than harder cords, but if you want decorator results, consider using it. The lamp cover shown on the front cover is a sleeve net made of cable cord.

Figuring Sizes

To work out the proportions of gauge size to mesh number for something like this lamp cover, first determine the circumference by measuring around the object. Divide the circumference by the number of mesh you wish to use to get the approximate diagonal measure of each mesh, assuming the net is hung square. Knowing the diagonal measure, you can determine which gauge size to use from the chart on page 21.

Consider a curved lamp cover as a series of concentric circles to figure the descending series of gauges to use. Or, determine the gauge size you wish to use at the greatest circumference. Look up the diagonal measure for that gauge on the chart and divide the diagonal measure into the circumference to determine the number of loops to make.

Making the Net

Since you are eventually going to discard the headrope used here, its size and length are optional—12″ to 24″ is plenty long and #21 or #36 seine twine are equally good.

Drive two finishing nails about 8″ apart into your work board. Use a bowline knot and a clove hitch to secure the headrope cord between the two nails (Illus. 39 shows how to tie these knots). Fill your shuttle with the $\frac{3}{32}''$ diameter soft cable cord and clove hitch the shuttle cord onto this headrope, leaving at least a 20″ tail. Go around

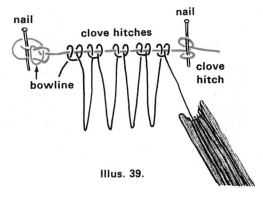

Illus. 39.

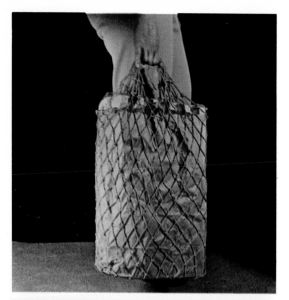

Illus. 40 (top left). Instructions for making this handy shopping bag appear on pages 40 to 44.

Illus. 41 (above). A book bag, like the one shown here, is a convenient way to carry books, note-books, or other flat objects.

Illus. 42 (bottom left). Although used here as a camping bag, this netted carrier could be useful to transport a variety of goods. Instructions begin on page 32.

Illus. 43. Catching fish will be a double pleasure if you use a home-made hand-held net such as as the one shown here.

Illus. 44. Use a large game fish net, like the one here, to land larger fish.

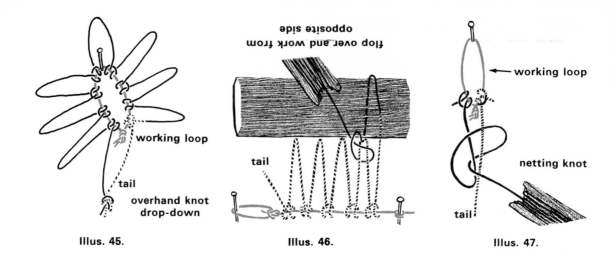

working loop

flop over and work from
opposite side

tail

Illus. 45.

Illus. 46.

← working loop

netting knot

tail

tail

overhand knot
drop-down

Illus. 47.

Illus. 48.

the 3″ gauge as usual, and clove hitch to the headrope again, repeating for 14 loops (see Illus. 39).

Note that it is possible to net straight from a single headrope just as you did from a double one, always working the netting from left to right (see Illus. 46).

Forming the Working Loop

For the lamp cover, you want to sleeve net. Form the working loop for this project by taking the headrope off the nails and tying the ends of the headrope together with an overhand knot (see Illus. 45). Tie the tail and the shuttle cord together to form the 15th loop, just as you do for a grommet start. You will have a fairly large oval which you will have to move along over a nail or other pivoting device, as shown in Illus. 48. When you are finished netting, you can untie the overhand knot and remove the headrope/working loop completely.

Net the first row (which is at the bottom of the completed shade) as you have learned (see Illus. 46 and 47), on a 3″ gauge, the 2nd row on a $2\frac{1}{2}$″ gauge, the 3rd row on a 2″ gauge, the 4th row on a $1\frac{3}{4}$″ gauge, and the 5th row on a $1\frac{1}{2}$″ gauge.

Closing the Bottom

After you have finished netting, there are a number of possible methods of closing the middle of the bottom (last netted row) of the lamp cover, or of bags or other shapes you work from the top down. The simplest is just to run the tail through the last row of loops and tie it and the shuttle cord together in a double overhand knot, gathering the net as close as you wish. (Use this method for

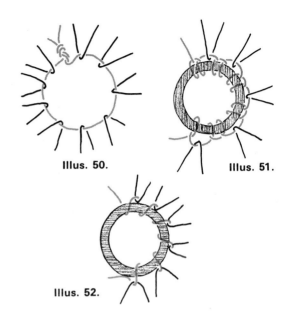

Illus. 50. Illus. 51.

Illus. 52.

the lamp cover.) If you wish to close the first netted row instead of the last, and there is no tail, use a separate piece of cord to do the same thing (see Illus. 50).

Another method of closing you could use is to lash the last row of loops to a metal or plastic ring, using the tail or a separate string and double half hitches between each loop (see Illus. 51).

An even simpler closing is lacing through each loop with the tail if it is available or with a separate lacing cord if it is not. You can also do this over a wrapped ring if you dislike seeing another material, such as metal or plastic, with your netting. Leave a tail from the separate wrapping cord. Wrap all around the ring and then lace all around (see Illus. 52). Tie the two ends of the cord together.

Illus. 49. As you net, your work should look like this.

29

Illus. 53. Instead of buying a new hammock each year, to replace the worn-out one of the previous summer, why not learn to make your own? Instructions begin on page 45.

Illus. 54. Rather than purchase a new frame, make your hammock to fit any frame you already have available.

30

Illus. 55. What experts your family will be if you have your own back-yard pitch-back for ball practice. This pitch-back utilizes the square-mesh technique of netting.

Illus. 56. Scrap pieces of net in various colors are a good source of materials for creative collages. Combine the net with different items, such as the simple wooden fish shown here, to produce different thematic pictures. Mount the collage on a canvas board and then place the entire creation into a ready-made frame.

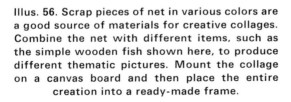

Tassels

Wrapped tassels were used to decorate the bottom of the lamp cover. To make tassels, just loop three or four strands of cord over the bottom mesh and wrap as shown in Illus. 57. Trim off the bottom of the tassels.

You can create some unusual effects for your tassels with certain cords. Try steaming them, for instance. In some cords, steaming fuzzes them up quite attractively. If you use braided nylon, on the other hand, you can separate the strands of the braid and then steam them to straighten them out.

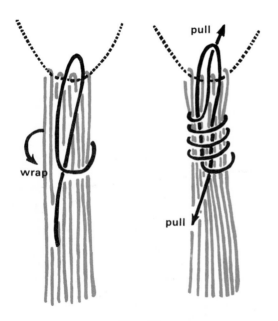

Illus. 57.

Camping Bag

Materials:
> #21 cotton seine twine
> $\frac{3}{4}''$ diameter plastic ring
> $2\frac{1}{2}''$ gauge
> $1\frac{1}{4}''$ gauge

Light-weight, hardwearing, adaptable and comfortable containers are often required for collecting and transporting clothing and equipment around camp and on vacation. In designing any container, you must consider the shape and size of the things to be contained. The camper's helper shown in Illus. 42 can easily accommodate a light bedding roll or beach blanket, towels and bathing suits. It also makes a good sized utility bag. Such a bag takes up very little room empty, but can expand to collect a lot of dirty clothes, ready for the next laundry stop.

The bag shown in Illus. 42 was made from the top down, though you could also make it by the grommet starting method, from the bottom up.

Cast on 23 mesh loops using the $2\frac{1}{2}''$ gauge on a single headrope (see page 25). Form the headrope into a working loop and tie the shuttle cord to the tail to make the 24th loop. Work circular straight for 25 rows, using the $1\frac{1}{4}''$ gauge.

Decreasing

To decrease, hold the gauge up to the loops from the previous row as for netting. Bring the shuttle cord over and around the gauge and through the loop of that mesh *and* of the adjacent mesh. Then proceed to throw the cord over to the left and pull and roll as for a regular netting

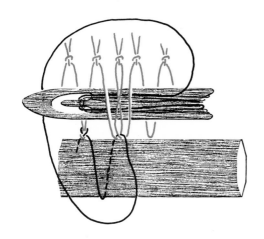

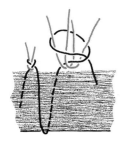

Illus. 58. Decreasing.

knot (see Illus. 58). This makes one knot netted into two loops simultaneously, reducing the total number of meshes on the gauge.

In the 26th row, decrease four times, evenly spaced around the circumference, leaving 20 loops. In the 27th row, decrease four times, leaving 16 loops. In the 28th row, decrease seven times, leaving 9 loops, Tie these remaining loops to a plastic ring with the tail (see Illus. 51). Tie off and clip the ends.

Drawstring Closure

Sennit Braids

Twine the same size as used to make a net bag is not usually suitable as a single strand for a drawstring closure. Using a larger twine, on the other hand, may not always be practical. There is another solution, at once practical and attractive—braid. You can use a standard 3-strand flat braid, but it may be somewhat small for your purposes. A 4-strand round (sennit) braid is an improvement and, once you have mastered the technique, is easy to make. An 8-strand sennit braid, shown in Illus. 42, was used for this project.

First practice making a 4-strand braid to learn the technique. Start with two cords in your left hand and two in your right. You are going to alternate hand and position in a specific order. This is a round sennit braid so the working cord always goes around behind the braid first. Take

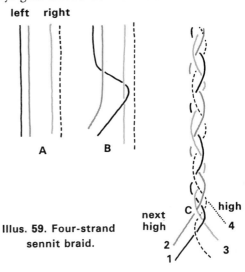

Illus. 59. Four-strand sennit braid.

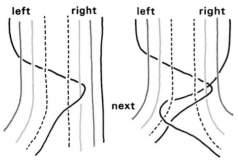

left   right   left   right

next

Illus. 60. Eight-strand sennit braid.

the outside strand on the left around, behind and forward between the two strands on the right (see Illus. 59 B). Bring it back to the left hand, this time to the low position (see Illus. 59B). Now take the outside strand on the right around, behind and forward between the two strands on the left. Bring it back to the low position on the right. Repeat the left-hand sequence and then repeat the right-hand sequence (see Illus. 59C). You have made one complete move, easily seen if you use different colors. (If you want to experiment with color, use one color in the high positions, a contrasting one for both low positions. Or start a different combination by alternating the colors straight across.)

An 8-strand sennit braid only looks more complicated. The technique is still the same: high strand around, behind and through the middle of the opposite side, return to low position on the starting side (see Illus. 60). You alternate sides the same way, though it is more difficult to keep the order of the four strands in each hand correct. If you ever have to stop for anything, pin the strands down in order. Picking out the high strand to determine which hand is next is not hard if you fan out both sets of cords. The

8-strand braid shown in Illus. 61 was done with four colors, the same as the diagram shows.

To make sure you will have a long enough drawstring, multiply the gauge size used for the major part of the bag by two to get the stretched dimension, then by the number of mesh in the bag. In this example, that is $1\frac{1}{4}'' \times 2 = 2\frac{1}{2}'' \times 24$ mesh $= 72''$. You are never going to pull a net bag all the way open, but braiding the cord uses up some length and you want the tasseled ends to stay clear of the drawstring loops, so your finished length should be pretty close to that 72". Allowing 2" and 2" for two tasseled ends plus 2" per foot (approximately) for take up in 8-strand braiding, you will be safe to cut your cords for the drawstring for this bag about 88" long.

You can finish any braided drawstring with a wrapped and tasseled end (see page 32).

Illus. 61. Eight-strand sennit braid.

Large Game Fish

Landing Net

Materials:

#18 treated cotton seine twine or nylon
birch or maple dowel, 1″ in diameter
oak block for tongue, 5/4 (standard stock) ×
    $1\frac{1}{2}$″ × 4″ long
solid aluminum rod 6 feet long, $\frac{3}{8}$″ in diameter
brass ring, 1″ in diameter
four bolts with nuts, 2″ long
$\frac{1}{4}$″ diameter hanger bolt with wood threads
1 fence staple
$1\frac{1}{4}$″ gauge
$1\frac{1}{2}$″ gauge
$\frac{1}{4}$″ drill bit
C-clamps and/or vice
hacksaw and file
leather thong

If your next camping trip is in pursuit of large game fish, you may want to prepare for it by making your own large landing net (see Illus. 44). You will have no excuse for losing that prize fish with a net this large!

Using the $1\frac{1}{2}$″ gauge, cast on 39 loops onto a single headrope, leaving a tail 48″ long. Form the headrope into a working loop and knot the tail to the shuttle cord to make the 40th mesh loop. Work 17 rows circular straight. Change to the $1\frac{1}{4}$″ gauge.

In the 18th row, decrease 10 times (evenly spaced) so that you have 30 loops. In the 19th row, decrease 10 more times so that you have 20 loops. In the 20th row, decrease 10 more times

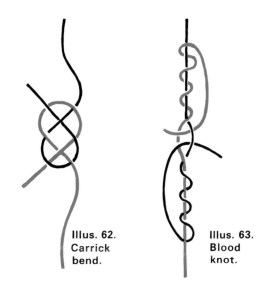

Illus. 62.
Carrick
bend.

Illus. 63.
Blood
knot.

until you have 10 loops. In the 21st row, decrease to five loops.

Because this net is so large, you will certainly need to refill your shuttle and join the old and new ends. You can use one of the methods of joining previously described (see pages 11 and 20), you can use the carrick bend, which was actually used for the net in Illus. 44, or you can use the extra strong blood knot, which is better for use with smaller twine.

You can tie the carrick bend neatly in any size cord. To tie it, form a loop in one end as shown in Illus. 62. Thread the other cord around the first one, going over and under in sequence as shown. Pull to tighten.

To make the blood knot, follow Illus. 63. First lay the old cord alongside the new one so they are parallel. Wrap one end over the other three times. Bring the end down between the splice and

Illus. 64. Lash the last five loops to a wrapped brass ring.

parts last longer if they are completely finished with preservative, apply a protective coating before assembling the handle.

Use the hanger bolt to fasten the tongue to the handle. This is easily done if you drill matching pilot holes straight into the end of the handle and straight into the end of the tongue first; start the hanger bolt in the handle, then start the tongue on the other end of it. Continue rotating both parts until they come together.

Clamp the rod frame in position and drill for bolts. Fasten the frame to handle and tongue assembly temporarily with the bolts and nuts. Put a board across the tip end of the rod frame. Clamp it down securely. Holding at the ends of the rod raise the handle to bend the tip into the

hold it. Repeat the same action with the other end. This leaves an opening at the junction between the two wraps. Put the ends through this opening. Pull the old cord and the new cord away from each other, thus tightening the knot.

Finish the net by lashing the five remaining loops to a wrapped brass ring, 1″ in diameter, as described on page 29 (see Illus. 51 and 64). Remove the headrope.

Making the Handle

First, bend the aluminum rod to the shape shown in Illus. 65, enlarging the pattern to full size (each square equals 1″). Make the tongue from the oak block, following the pattern shown on page 22, to fit this metal frame. Because wooden

Illus. 65.   **each square equals 1″**

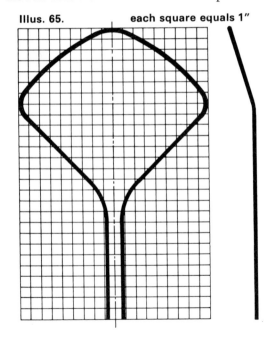

turned-up position indicated in Illus. 65. Unclamp the rod frame, remove the frame from handle assembly and thread the frame through the top loops of the net, reserving one mesh to fasten later. Replace the frame with the net attached, fastening it with epoxy glue and the bolts to the handle and tongue assembly. Adjust the net and staple the one free mesh to the end of the middle of the tongue using the fence staple.

Apply protective nose wrapping around the frame, catching in the mesh opposite the one you just stapled (see Illus. 66). (See page 13 for wrapping detail.)

Cut off the ends of the bolts with a hacksaw and file smooth so they are flush with the nuts. Then wrap the handle double to cover the bolt heads and nuts.

Illus. 66. Wrap around the nose of the frame, catching one mesh as shown.

Drill a hole through the end of the handle parallel to the frame. Thread the thong through the hole and tie the ends together.

Your large landing net is ready to use.

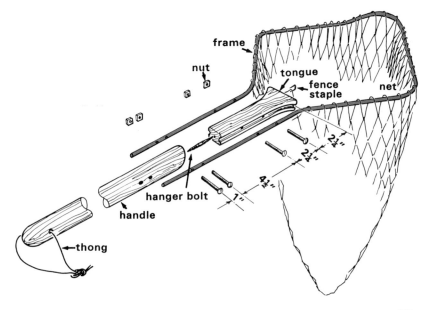

Illus. 67. Assembly of large game fish landing net.

frame

nut

tongue

fence staple

net

hanger bolt

handle

thong

$2\frac{1}{4}''$

$2\frac{1}{4}''$

$2\frac{1}{4}''$

$4\frac{1}{2}''$

$1''$

Mini-Hammock

Illus. 68. This mini-hammock is a unique toy
"box."

Materials:

    #9 cotton seine twine
    #36 cotton seine twine
    two brass rings, 2″ in diameter
    $1\frac{1}{2}$″ gauge
    $1\frac{1}{4}$″ gauge
    1″ gauge
    raffia needle

For toys, pajamas or whatever you wish, the seamen's storage net is a practical and decorative solution. The size, of course, is variable but remember: if you make the mesh too large, things will fall out.

To cast on something solid and permanent and not flexible (such as the brass ring used in this mini-hammock) requires a different method than you have learned. Clove hitching (two half hitches made in the same direction), shown in Illus. 69, is the most straightforward solution whether you are working with brass rings or ring handles for a handbag or a ready-made ring for a ring start bottom. You can also use a half hitch combined with a reverse half hitch (see Illus. 70) for a more

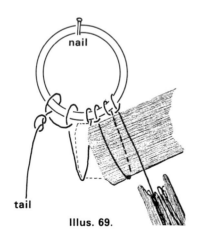

Illus. 69.

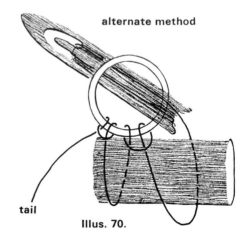

alternate method

Illus. 70.

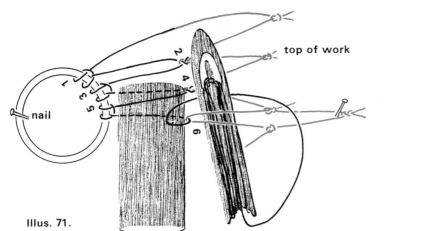

Illus. 71.

Illus. 72.

decorative start, although mesh loops cast on this way seem to slip more.

To cast on by this method, first hook the ring over a nail. Bring the shuttle under the ring, up through it, and down to the left of the tail which should be 6″ or 7″ long for this project. Repeat for the second hitch, but this time, come down to the left of the first part and over the face of the 1½″ gauge and up the back, repeating the double half hitch.

Cast on 12 loops in this way, using the #9 twine and the 1½″ gauge. Turn your work and net one row on the 1¼″ gauge. Turn your work again and, using the 1″ gauge, net 11 rows. On the 12th row, increase two times to 14 mesh. In the 14th row, increase to 16 mesh, in the 17th row, increase to 18 mesh and work straight to the 21st row in which you decrease two times back to 16 mesh. In the 24th row, decrease to 14 mesh, and in the 26th row, decrease back to the original 12 mesh.

Work straight to the 40th row, change from the 1″ to the 1¼″ gauge, work one row. In the 42nd row, use the 1½″ gauge and cast off to the ring.

To cast off to the ring, you need two nails set as shown in Illus. 71 so that the distance established between the ring and the loop you are netting into equals that of the gauge width. Take the shuttle cord and clove hitch around the ring as shown at #1 in Illus. 71. Step so you are facing the net loops and work the netting knot at #2. Turn around and clove hitch to the ring as shown at #3, move back around and make a netting knot at #4, moving the net over so that the mesh you knot into is hung on the nail. Move towards the ring and make a clove hitch at #5, and so on. Your hammock should hang evenly now.

Tie an overhand knot in the tail, tight up against the ring. To give a neat finish to the attachment at the ring, thread the raffia needle with the tail and weave through, forming a sort

39

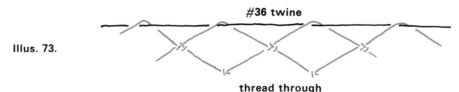

#36 twine

Illus. 73.

thread through

of hammock clew (see Illus. 72). Bring the weaving thread through the attaching loops twice. Bring it up above the first line woven and take it part way through again. Bring the cord out the back, unravel it and, with the needle, run one ply over a couple of cords. Tie the single ply to the remaining ones.

Repeat this at the other end, cutting the shuttle off so that you have about 6″ left to work with.

Shopping Bag

Materials:
  #18 cotton seine twine
  #72 cotton seine twine
  $\frac{3}{4}$″ gauge
  $1\frac{1}{4}$″ gauge

If you ever wished that shopping bags had something more comfortable than the harsh single-string handles most shopping bags have, why not make your own net shopping bag, light enough to take with you and comfortable enough so that you can carry quite a load without noticing it? While many shopping bags are made with bone or metal ring handles, the soft wrapped handle is certainly more comfortable to hold. In addition, you can stuff the whole bag into a pocket to carry empty.

The bag described here and shown in Illus. 40

To give some shape to the mini-hammock, run a line of #36 twine around the edge, threading it through the side loops as shown in Illus. 73. The simplest way to complete the circuit is to take the #36 twine right through the end rings and to tie the two ends together in a tassel at the front of the hammock or as inconspicuously as possible at the back. Tightening the #36 twine shapes the mini-hammock.

is sized to carry an average grocery sack comfortably. If you want to pack your groceries in a paper sack or bag first, instead of putting the articles directly into the net, put the net bag down first, open the handles out and arrange the bottom neatly. Set the paper sack in place on top of the net bag, then pack the paper sack and pull the net bag up over it. Walk off in comfort.

In an ecological effort to save paper, refuse the paper sack and pack the net bag yourself, putting largest and heaviest articles on the bottom, lighter crushables on top. If you bought anything small enough to slip through the mesh, accept a small paper bag for that. Otherwise, net is a natural for store trips. You will probably even want to make two!

Start this shopping bag on a single headrope by casting on 23 loops of the #18 twine, using the

$1\frac{1}{4}''$ gauge. Form the headrope into a working loop and make the 24th mesh by tying the shuttle cord and the tail together. Leave a tail about 30" long. Work circular straight for 14 rows.

On the 15th row, decrease in 8 mesh so you have a total of 16 mesh. Remove the net from the headrope loop and tie off the tail.

The bottom is seamed closed to give a neat, angular shape to the bag, as shown in Illus. 77.

Seaming

To close the bottom of the shopping bag, or if you do not like to work circular, or you want to make different shapes, you must learn to seam. Before you learn to seam, however, you must know how to net backwards—that is, from right to left.

Working Backwards

To net from right to left is handy in working large pieces where turning each row would be time-consuming and tiring, when walking around the net is impractical and in seaming, which requires alternating from right to left and left to right. It is not complicated to net "backwards."

To begin with, first take the shuttle cord behind the gauge, then over the front of the gauge, then from front to back through the mesh loop at the top of the gauge (see Step 1 in Illus. 74). Hold the shuttle cord under your thumb as in normal knotting, but throw the loop to the right, over the two parts of the mesh you are knotting into. Bring the shuttle to the right, under the mesh and over the loop just thrown, as shown in Step 2 in Illus. 74. Pull the shuttle cord down to the left to tighten the knot, as shown in Step 3 in Illus. 74.

Completing the Seam

You need two nails the right distance apart (see page 39) to produce a seam the same size as your other mesh. You recall that to net evenly requires a holding point directly above the mesh loop you want to net into. To make a seam, you must move both sides of the net to be joined along so

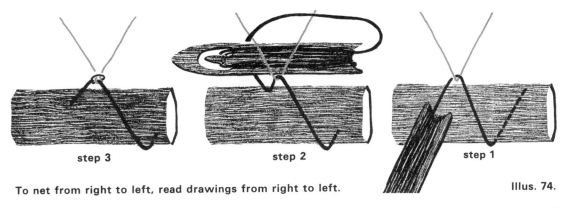

step 3   **step 2**   **step 1**

To net from right to left, read drawings from right to left.

Illus. 74.

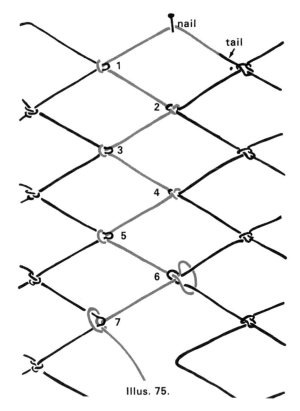

Illus. 75.

knot #3, then net from left to right at #4, and so on. Remember: the shuttle should always pull the knot tight in the same direction as the seam is progressing.

A handy hint for what joins what is: the zig-zag shape of one side of the net would fit into the zig-zag shape of the other side if you moved the two sides horizontally together.

To close the bottom of this shopping bag, take the shuttle cord to the adjacent mesh loops as shown in Illus. 77, forming a triangle as indicated. Continue the seam as described above. Tie off the shuttle cord when you reach the end of the seam, forming another triangle as you did to start the seam.

Finishing the Shopping Bag

Now go to the top of the bag. Consider each side as 12 loops in a line parallel with the bottom

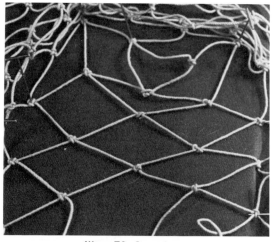

Illus. 76. Seaming.

that you always have something to pull the mesh against evenly.

Take a look at Illus. 75. Notice that the tail is used here to run the seam. To make a loop even with the others in the top row of the net, place the nail as shown to provide the right length. Net from right to left as described above at knot #1. It is easier to seam in this way if you turn your whole self to face the mesh you are knotting into. Do so and then net from left to right at knot #2. Turn yourself again and go from right to left at

42

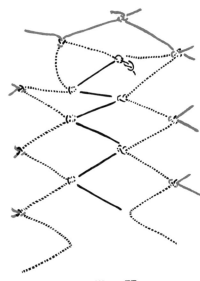

Illus. 77.

should be at the middle of the opposite side. Cut the #72 twine off about 5″ from this knot.

Loosen the knot and restart the #72 twine from the shuttle by running the new end back through the knot. (This is done to make the two sides symmetrical.) Repeat the netting pattern of the first side: net one mesh on the $\frac{3}{4}''$ gauge, three mesh on the $1\frac{1}{4}''$ gauge, four mesh on the $\frac{3}{4}''$ gauge, three mesh on the $1\frac{1}{4}''$ gauge and one more mesh on the $\frac{3}{4}''$ gauge. This brings you back where you started. Lay the finishing end back through the knot there, too.

Perhaps the easiest way to see what you are doing in making the handles is to run a working dowel through the top row of bag mesh along one side. There should be two groups of three long loops directly facing you. Number them in your mind as is shown in Illus. 78. Knot the #72 twine to loop #1, leaving about a 9″ tail. Carry the twine to loop #4 and knot again, leaving a loop large enough to get your hand through comfortably. Once you have determined this length, make each succeeding handle loop the same length.

Knot to loop #2 next, then to loop #5, back

seam you just made. Find the middle of the mesh of one side and attach the #72 twine with a netting knot. Work one mesh over the $\frac{3}{4}''$ gauge, then three mesh over the $1\frac{1}{4}''$ gauge, then four mesh over the $\frac{3}{4}''$ gauge, then three mesh over the $1\frac{1}{4}''$ gauge and one more over the $\frac{3}{4}''$ gauge. You

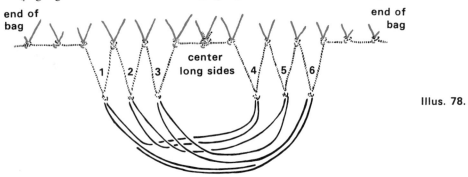

end of bag

center long sides

1 2 3 4 5 6

end of bag

Illus. 78.

43

Illus. 79. Cover the handles with alternating half hitches as shown here.

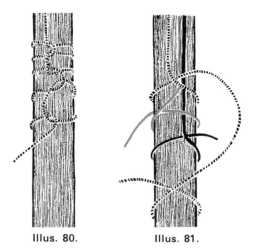

Illus. 80.   Illus. 81.

for one handle. Pull the ends of the #18 through the loop, tightening it around the gathered strands of #72. To make covering the handle easier, put the bottom of the three handle meshes over a nail and temporarily tie one set of handle cords in a bunch, making sure you include both cut ends in place to be covered. Work fairly tight, following Illus. 80, and cover an area 4″ to 5″ long at the middle of the handle loop.

Tie a square knot in the ends and, using a raffia needle, thread the ends up through the handle (see Illus. 82). Clip off.

You can also get rid of the cut ends of the #72 twine under the covering by first pulling each end out a bit, cutting it off and then gently pulling it back until it disappears. (If you want to do this, do it before clipping the #18 twine covering cords off.) Now finish the other handle the same way.

You are not, of course, limited in how many strands you decide to hitch. You may, for instance, choose to use three, as shown in Illus. 81, which gives a nice braided effect.

to loop #3 and finally to loop #6. Cut off the #72 twine, leaving about 9″ hanging free.

Turn the bag so the other side is facing you and repeat all this, taking care to make the two handles the same length.

The handles shown in Illus. 79 were covered with #18 twine doubled and worked in alternating half hitches. To do this, cut two 6-foot lengths of the #18 twine. Fold one in half. Lay this loop under the #72 twine forming the base

Illus. 82. Pull the end of the cord through the handle as shown.

Full-Size Hammock

Materials:

> #72 cotton seine twine
> nylon clothesline
> two $\frac{1}{4}''$ steel rings, $3\frac{1}{2}''$ in diameter
> oak spreaders, one 36" long, one 24" long;
>   5/4 × 5/4 stock
> 2" gauge
> hand or power drill for making holes $\frac{1}{4}''$ in
>   diameter through the oak
> board or plywood
> hammer and nails for clew jig

No book on netting is really complete without a hammock project. Construct your first full-size hammock by using an old metal frame from a lawn hammock, otherwise useless because the hammock that used to fit the frame has worn out. Then you need to select a cord that is comfortable and, for a first hammock, reasonably easy and quick to knot. The hammock in Illus. 53 was made with #72 cotton seine twine which is not as easy to knot tightly as smaller sizes, but is not hard to work.

The hammock shown is a bit too heavy to backpack, but not too heavy if you camp from a car or trailer. Just unhook the rings from the frame and take the hammock, plus a good amount of $\frac{3}{8}''$ manila rope, and look for two trees reasonably well positioned for slinging your hammock by the campfire.

To make the hammock pictured in Illus. 53, you need first of all to check the over-all dimension of your frame. The one shown measured 10' 8" from hook to hook. If yours is a lot longer, add a few rows of mesh and allow more length in the hammock clews. If yours is a lot shorter, shorten the clew lengths shown by 12" or 14" in the head clew and only 3" or 4" at the foot. Be sure to wait until you fasten the clew to the hammock to cut off the excess.

Cast on 12 mesh over a temporary single or double headrope. Work a few rows straight and transfer to a 1" working dowel if you wish. On row 12, increase one. On row 14, increase two mesh, equally spaced. On row 15, increase one more time to make a total of 16 mesh. Work straight to row 23, where you decrease two times to 14 mesh. Decrease one in row 25 and one in row 29 to return to 12 mesh. Work straight to your desired length, a total of 40 or 42 rows. Tie off.

Making the Mountings

Cut the oak 5/4 × 5/4 stock to the proper length. Drill $\frac{1}{4}''$ diameter holes as shown in Illus. 83, 3" center to center on the 36" long piece and 2" center to center on the 24" length. Drill an additional $\frac{1}{4}''$ hole immediately next to each end hole, making the last opening a rough oval. Round all edges, sand smooth and finish the wood with plastic varnish. If you have a countersink bit (which produces a bevelled edge around the top inside edge of the hole you drill) and want to take the time, it will save wear and tear on the mounting cords if you use it to ease top and bottom of each hole.

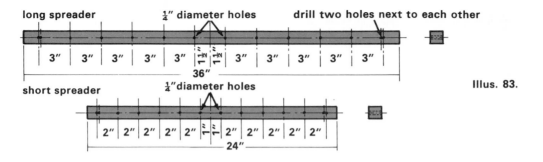

long spreader   ¼″ diameter holes   drill two holes next to each other

| 3″ | 3″ | 3″ | 3″ | 3″ | 1½″ | 1½″ | 3″ | 3″ | 3″ | 3″ | 3″ |

36″

short spreader   ¼″diameter holes

| 2″ | 2″ | 2″ | 2″ | 2″ | 1″ | 1″ | 2″ | 2″ | 2″ | 2″ | 2″ |

24″

Illus. 83.

Making the clews (the end lines by which you hang the hammock) requires a jig which is simply a temporary arrangement for holding the cords in a fan shape while you work on them. Any base you do not mind driving nails into will work. Place one nail at the middle of the top for the ring. Then drive 12 nails equally spaced (about 2″ apart gives you the space you need to weave the clew properly) on a line 36″ away from the first nail (see Illus. 84). (NOTE: Illus. 84 shows looping around a row of nails 24″ away from the first nail. This measurement will be for the foot clew.)

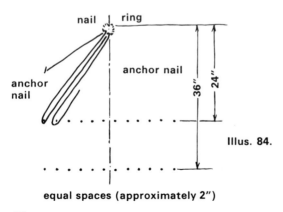

nail   ring

anchor nail

anchor nail

36″   24″

Illus. 84.

equal spaces (approximately 2″)

To set up your cord, measure off 24″ and drive a nail at the left-hand side to temporarily anchor this end (see Illus. 84). Measure off and cut 48 feet of #72 seine twine. Run this end up through the ring, down around the first nail, back up under and through the ring and repeat until you have a bight (loop) around each nail. Anchor the end around an additional nail. Check to make sure you have always come up under and through the ring, that you came around the nails in sequence and that the tension on the twine is about the same all over.

Use your gauge or a ruler as a tool to open a shed to weave the clew. (Shed is a weaving term which means the space between two sets of warp or lengthwise threads.) Because of the way you wound the twine around the ring, half the twine lines go up and half go down. Weave the gauge through flat to bring up the twine lines that are down. Turn the gauge on edge (see Illus. 85). Take the right-hand end of twine through the shed until it passes bight #2 (see Illus. 86). Take the left-hand end of twine through until it passes bight #11 (see Illus. 86). Take bight #1 and bight #12 and hook them up out of the way over the anchor nails.

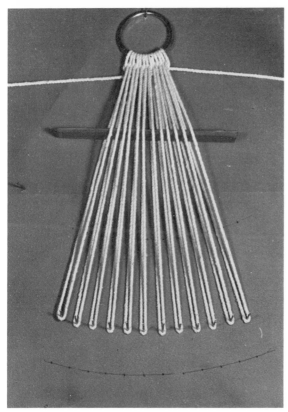

Illus. 85. Turn the gauge on edge to open a shed.

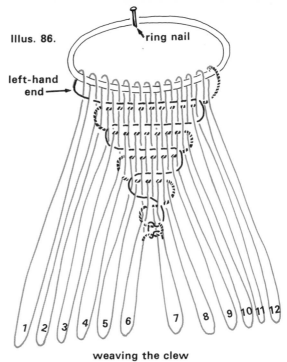

weaving the clew

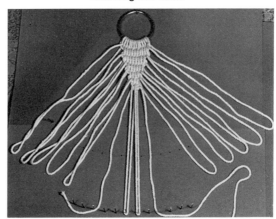

Illus. 87. Weave until only bights #6 and #7 are left.

Use the gauge again to bring up the alternate set of twine lines and weave both ends through as you did before, crossing in the middle of the open shed. Note that you only weave through the outside bight once each time and then drop it, while you weave both ends through all the other bights.

Continue to weave and drop until only the two middle bights are left, #6 and #7 (see Illus. 87).

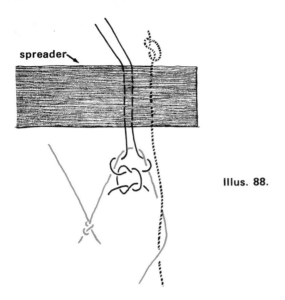

spreader

Illus. 88.

the tension on all the bights is as equal as you can get it. This is best done starting with bight #6, then #7, then #5, and so on, alternating from left side to right, working out from the middle of the head spreader.

For the foot end, lay the clew out flat and pull the bights through holes in the foot spreader and tie to matching hammock mesh as for the head. Unhook the head spreader from the frame. Hook the ring of the foot spreader clew to the foot hook on the hammock frame. Make any necessary adjustments.

Replace the head clew ring onto the hook of the hammock frame. The hammock will look like a figure 8. Run the nylon clothesline through the last (oval) hole on the head spreader, thread it through the edge mesh along that side of the hammock and through the oval hole on the foot spreader. Do the same with the nylon clothesline on the other side of the hammock.

Knot the head ends and pull up tight to the head spreader. Pull the free ends, first one then the other, to adjust the belly of the hammock. Tie temporarily at the foot spreader. Test the hammock for stretch and comfort. Work knots in side cords tight to keep the desired shape.

Nylon clothesline frays and unravels if it is not fused. When you knot each end above the head spreader, apply heat (with a lighter) to set the knots. Do the same at the foot after you have made and tested adjustments.

Note that you can adjust the hammock further by chain on most frames or by ropes around trees if you are not using a frame.

Lie back, relax and think up your next netting project.

Change the shed and tie a square knot between them. Stop the ends with an overhand knot. Take this clew off the nails and repeat the whole process for the foot clew, this time putting the original row of nails 24″ down from the ring nail.

Assembling the Hammock and Clews

Lay the head clew out flat. Pull each bight through the appropriate hole on the head spreader (Illus. 83). Lay the hammock out flat, matching up the bights and the top row of mesh loops. Cut each bight. Take the two cut ends of each bight through the matching mesh loop from back to front. Carry the ends around and behind and tie them in a square knot (see Illus. 88). Do not tighten up yet. Tie all the ends and then hang up the whole thing by the ring onto the hook of the frame. Make any necessary adjustments so that

48

Square Mesh Pitch-Back

Materials:

#36 cotton seine twine

4 pieces of aluminum tubing, each 1″ in diameter and 3 feet long

4 corner connectors for the aluminum tubing

2 pieces of solid aluminum rod, $\frac{3}{8}$″ in diameter and 4 feet long; for legs, have one end of each threaded (grooved) to accept:

> 2 nuts
>
> 2 wing nuts
>
> 8 washers
>
> 8 lock washers
>
> 8 tension springs, $\frac{1}{4}$″ in diameter by $1\frac{1}{2}$″ long
>
> 8 tension springs, $\frac{1}{4}$″ in diameter by 2″ long

brightly colored yarn or seam tape

drill bit $\frac{1}{8}$″ in diameter

drill bit for metal to clear $\frac{3}{8}$″ diameter thread

$1\frac{1}{2}$″ gauge

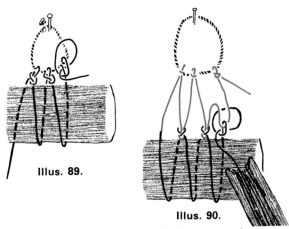

Illus. 89.

Illus. 90.

A pitch-back, suitable for back-yard ball tossing practice, requires less than a square yard of netting and a bit of framing. The one shown in Illus. 55 was made of aluminum tubing available in 6-foot lengths along with ready-made fittings to make the job simple. You can frame your pitch-back in wood and set it between two posts sunk into the ground, if that seems easier to you.

Square Meshing

Square meshing is no different from diamond meshing, except that the built-in selvage arrangement limits the movement of the net so that the mesh open square. You use the same shuttle, the same gauge, and the same method of knotting,

except that you purposely make the increase loop the "wrong" way, so it slides back down into position. The evenness of your work shows up more in square meshing than in diamond meshing, but both varieties have their place.

To commence square meshing, take a length of twine and tie it into a loop with a double overhand knot. Hang this supporting loop over a nail. Fill your shuttle and, leaving a short tail, tie the twine to the supporting loop. Come over and around the gauge stick as usual and knot again to the loop. Move over and around the gauge once more and knot to the supporting loop. Remove the gauge stick. You have two loops hanging (see Illus. 89).

Turn your work over and, using the techniques you have already learned, tie the netting knot into these two loops. Go again into the second loop and tie a netting knot the "wrong" way as shown in Illus. 90, pulling up a loop within the second loop so there is room to work the shuttle through.

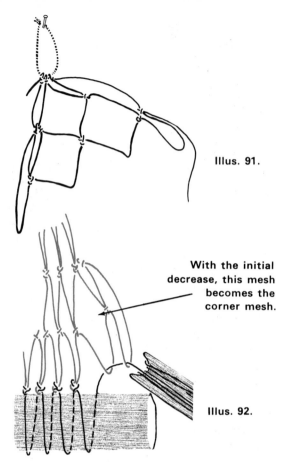

Illus. 91.

With the initial
decrease, this mesh
becomes the
corner mesh.

Illus. 92.

each row until you are left with only two loops and the shuttle cord. Carry the shuttle through the last two loops and work the netting knot just as you do in diamond meshing. You should see the corner form as you pull the knot tight (see Illus. 92 and 93).

Go back to the first corner you made. Remove the supporting loop from the nail, untie it, and pull out of the starting mesh. Take the tail you left and tie it through the two loops you have there, just as you did the two on the final corner.

Weave a target area in the middle of the net (see Illus. 94 for detail), using a dozen or more strands of brightly colored yarn or a length of seam tape.

(You can use this same weaving technique to decorate a simple shawl or café curtains of hand-tied square meshing.)

To work rectangular, as for a shawl, alternately increase and decrease, row after row. In other words, on the 13th row, increase; on the 14th row, decrease, and so on, alternately increasing at the end of one row and decreasing at the

Turn your work and do one more row the same way, increasing in the last loop. Now open up what you have done so far and check it against Illus. 91.

Following the square meshing method, work down 23 rows, increasing at the end of each row. At the end of the 24th row, commence decreasing to form the first corner. Decrease at the end of

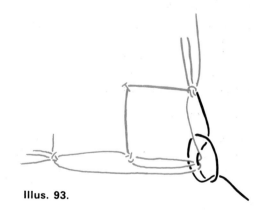

Illus. 93.

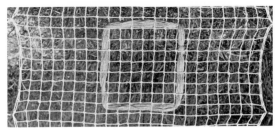

Illus. 94. Weave a target area in the middle of the pitch-back.

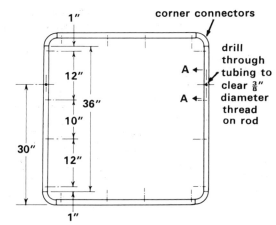

Illus. 95. Dimensions of the frame, with indications where to drill into the tubing.

end of the next. This produces a long, narrow piece. Because alternating in this way can get confusing, you could mark the decrease side with a bit of yarn to help remember which is which.

When you have reached the length desired (three or four feet is about right for a scarf, five feet or more for a shawl) and you want to turn another corner, decrease at the end of every row until you reach the final corner. Tie off as shown in Illus. 93.

Making the Frame

To make the frame, first drill the holes for the springs as shown in Illus. 95. Then insert the corner connectors, making sure all the spring holes are on the inside of the frame. To bend the legs, use a vice and take care not to mash the threading.

Use two of the 2" springs in each corner to attach the net to the frame. Do the diagonally opposite corners first. Then with the 1½" springs in the intermediate holes, attach the sides of the net. In attaching each spring to the net, make

Illus. 96. Use springs to attach the net to the frame.

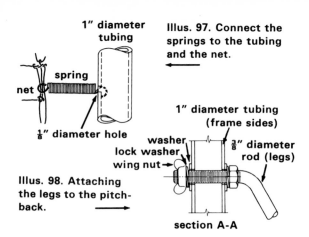

1" diameter tubing

Illus. 97. Connect the springs to the tubing and the net.

spring

net

⅛" diameter hole

1" diameter tubing (frame sides)

washer
lock washer
wing nut →

⅜" diameter rod (legs)

Illus. 98. Attaching the legs to the pitch-back.

section A-A

sure you hook over all of the cords in the selvage at that point.

With the frame face down, drill the holes for the supports (one for each leg) straight through the tubing. Run the plain nut and a lock washer and a washer on the threaded end. Put the legs through the frame and fasten at the front side using a washer, lock washer and wing nut (see Illus. 98). Take the pitch-back to the practice field and stick the legs into the ground firmly. Throwing into the net should not knock it over.

Tennis Net

Because a regulation tennis net requires a piece of net 280 meshes long and 20 meshes wide, based on a $1\frac{1}{2}''$ regulation square, you should only attempt to make one after you have achieved a fair amount of speed and regularity in netting.

First make the net, following the instructions for square meshing on page 49. To finish the net, first fold a piece of canvas the length of the net, as shown in Illus. 99. Then sew the net in between the folded-over piece as shown. Run a rope or piece of wire cable through this to hang the net from the posts. Hold the net taut with a second rope or piece of wire cable, run from the post to a metal grommet set in the ends of the folded canvas.

To complete the bottom of the net, clove hitch the net around a rope run from post to post, as shown in Illus. 100.

You can make badminton and volleyball nets in a similar manner.

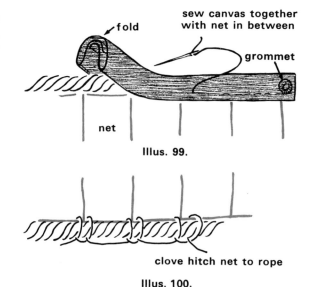

fold

sew canvas together with net in between

grommet

net

Illus. 99.

clove hitch net to rope

Illus. 100.

Macramé and Net Planter

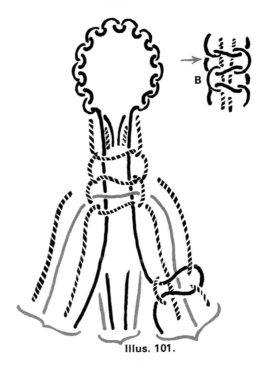

Materials:
  #3 braided nylon
  #2 braided nylon
  T-pins
  pinning surface for macramé
  3″ gauge
  1¼″ gauge

You can quickly, easily and economically—in both time and material—net a bag-shaped container, tied from a grommet start, for almost any plant pot. Netting, however, does not make the best straps, but macramé designs are very well suited to this portion of a hanging planter. An elementary planter design, combining simple macramé with netting, is shown on the front cover.

Cast on 11 loops of #3 nylon on a double headrope, using the 1¼″ gauge, and form into a grommet, tying the tail to the shuttle cord to form the 12th loop. Work 5 rows circular straight. Change to the 3″ gauge and work one more row. Tie off securely.

When using braided nylon, as you did here, you may want to set all your knots with heat. To do so, you use an ordinary household iron. Place aluminum foil between the iron and the nylon to keep any melted nylon off your good iron. Then simply iron the knots.

Making the Straps

Cut six cords of the #2 nylon, each 7 feet long. Set two cords aside and pin the other four in

Illus. 101.

position so you can tie a sennit (series) of square knots about 2″ long in the middle. Fold the group in half through the sennit and pin the loop to a working surface. Take one working cord and one core cord from each end of the sennit and tie one square knot in the new sets as shown in Illus. 101. Set in one of the two remaining cords on each side as shown. Tie an additional half-knot to keep it there.

Re-section the 12 cords resulting into three groups of four cords each and tie three square knots in each group. Alternate the knot position for four rows, then work a square knot sennit of eight knots in each group.

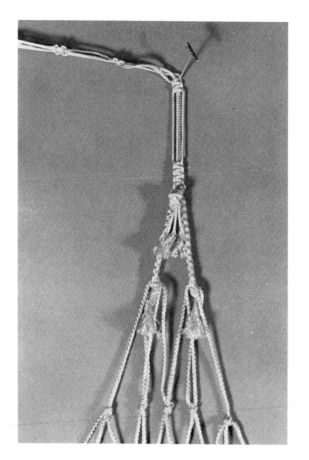

For the planter on the front cover, spaced pairs of square knots were then made down the straps (pin each strap carefully to maintain accurate spacing). You may vary this arrangement, of course, perhaps adding beads or spacing all the knots evenly. Finish each strap at the bottom with a group of four square knots.

Finishing the Planter

Cut six lengths of #2 nylon, each 18″ long, and six lengths, each 8″ long. Gather the cords in groups of four, with two long and two short in each group. Fold one group in half and lay it in across the core cords, under the working cords at the bottom of each strap. Work two square knots and an overhand knot in each strap to hold the other cords fast.

Then work a square knot sennit in the laid-in strands both ways from the strap. Gather two adjacent mesh from the netted portion in each set. Make an overhand knot to secure. Do the same at the end of each strap. Heat-set or use white (Elmer's) glue to secure the overhand knots. Set your pot in place and your planter is ready to be hung.

Illus. 102.

Netted Sculpture

The sculptural form shown on the front cover utilizes techniques shown in this book but also introduces a concept perhaps unfamiliar to netting, the interpenetration of one net-contained space through another netted shape. It is easy enough to get one shape inside another in circular netting, but to make one net penetrate another requires first that the mesh openings on one net are aligned with the mesh loops on the other when both nets are in their final (stretched) position. It is easiest if you have the same number of mesh openings on one net as you have mesh loops on the other, though you could have half as many loops and penetrate every other mesh just as well. Working this out is pretty much a matter of guesswork.

For the sculpture on the front cover, the yellow shape was worked first in #9 cotton seine twine from a grommet start. Both rings were wrapped and inserted temporarily so the size of the top part of the blue net (also made from #9 seine twine) could be determined. The blue net was started from a grommet with 8 mesh worked circular straight for about 12 rows, then increased rapidly to 24 mesh, the same number as there are on the yellow net at that point.

The blue net was then "tried on" for size inside the yellow net. The rings were removed and the blue net was brought through the yellow one, one mesh at a time, netting each mesh loop in the usual way, capturing the yellow mesh within the blue mesh loops as each was formed. The 3″ gauge was used on both nets to work the rows of interpenetration. The technique is simply one of working on the second net, which requires relaxing the first net. You cannot net accurately with the first net in the stretched position.

A few more rows on the blue net brought it out to the larger diameter of the blue-wrapped ring. A second blue net goes from a grommet start at the bottom of the sculpture to the same ring. All three rings are simply lashed to the nets. The tennis balls in the bottom weight the sculpture enough to stretch the nets taut and hold the top ball captured inside the blue net.

The whole sculpture is hung on a large bead on an overhand-knotted loop taken through the grommet top of the inside net, then through the grommet of the outside net.

There are a lot more possibilities for you to explore to net for fun. What happens if you start with a grommet and take half the loops up for one circular shape, the other half down? Can you put a double selvage in the middle of a net, use half the mesh to continue one shape, the other half to start another one? Combining netting with macramé and other textile techniques is still another media-mix to explore both for sculpture and for practical solutions to specific designs. Possibilities along these lines are limitless. What can you figure out?

Index